A MODERN METHOD FOR GUITAR
by WILLIAM LEAVITT

Volume I

It is important that the following material be covered in consecutive order. The index on page 126 is for reference purposes only and will prove valuable for review or concentration on specific techniques.

Outline
(Section I)

Berklee Press Publications
P.O. Box 489, Boston, MA 02199

SECTION ONE

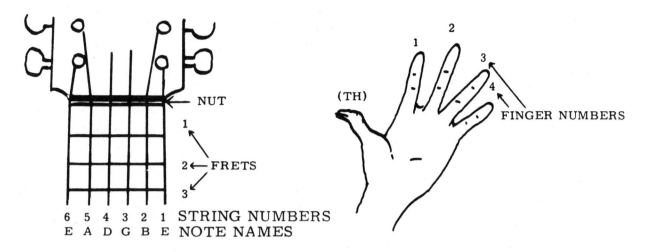

NUT

FRETS

FINGER NUMBERS

(TH)

1 2 3 4

6 5 4 3 2 1   STRING NUMBERS
E A D G B E   NOTE NAMES

TO TUNE THE GUITAR: (using piano or pitch pipe)

1. Tune the open 1st string to the first E above middle C...
2. Press the 2nd string down at the fifth fret and tune (2nd stg.) until it sounds exactly the same as the open 1st string.......
3. Press the 3rd string down at the fourth fret and tune (3rd stg.) until it sounds exactly the same as the open 2nd string...
4. Press 4th string at fifth fret... tune to open 3rd string.....
5.   "   5th   "   "   "   " ... "   "   "   4th   " .....
6.   "   6th   "   "   "   " ... "   "   "   5th   " .....

THE STAFF: consists of 5 lines and 4 spaces, and is divided into MEASURES by BAR LINES.....

(lines)   (spaces)   MEASURE

bar line   bar line   double bar line

CLEF SIGN: Guitar music is written in the TREBLE (or "G") clef, and the number of sharps (♯) or flats (♭) found next to the clef sign indicate the KEY SIGNATURE. (to be explained more fully at a later time...)

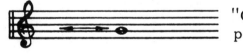

"G" clef shows the position of the note G

"COMMON" TIME VALUES OF THE NOTES:

whole note   half notes   quarter notes   eighth notes (in groups).....(or singlely)

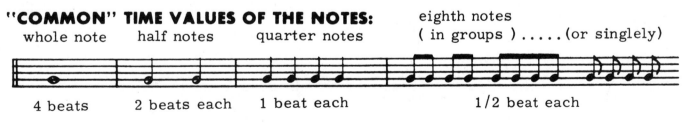

4 beats   2 beats each   1 beat each   1/2 beat each

Continued on next page

TIME SIGNATURES: Next to the clef sign (at the beginning of a composition) are found two numbers (like a fraction) or a symbol which represents these numbers. The top number tells how many beats (or counts) in a measure, and the bottom number indicates what kind of note gets one beat.

EXAMPLE: 🔢 means four quarters, or four beats per measure with a quarter note receiving one beat, or count. The symbol is...**C**

Notes In The First Position

(No sharps or flats.. KEY of C Major)

Order of the notes going up the scale
A B C D E F G, A B C D E F G, A B etc..
Start at any point, read left to right

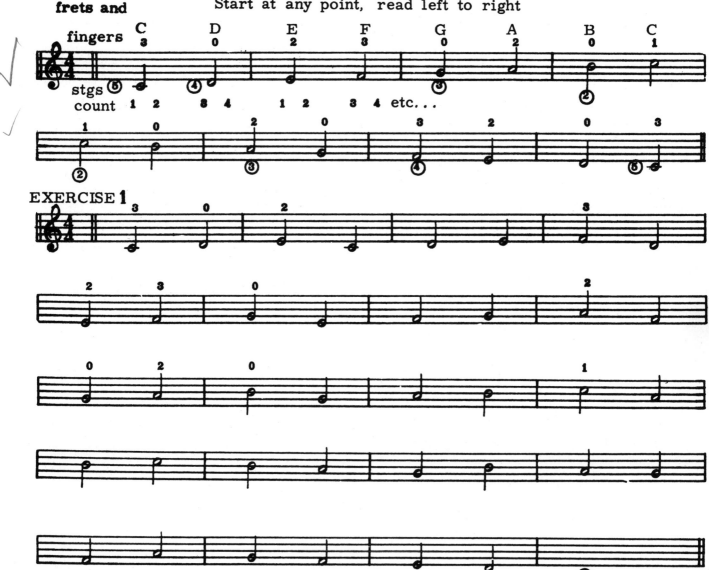

count 1 2 3 4

"READ" the notes, NOT the fingering, as these
numbers will eventually be omitted....

EXERCISE **2**

hold notes down

EXERCISE **3**

EXERCISE **4**

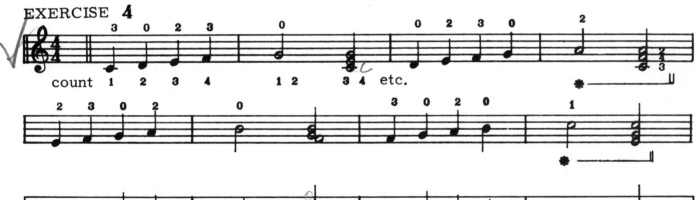

count 1 2 3 4   1 2   3 4 etc.

Sea To Sea (duet)

(1st Guitar)

(2nd Guitar)

10/17/05

Note And Chord Review

(Regular review of all material is a must!)

EXERCISE 7

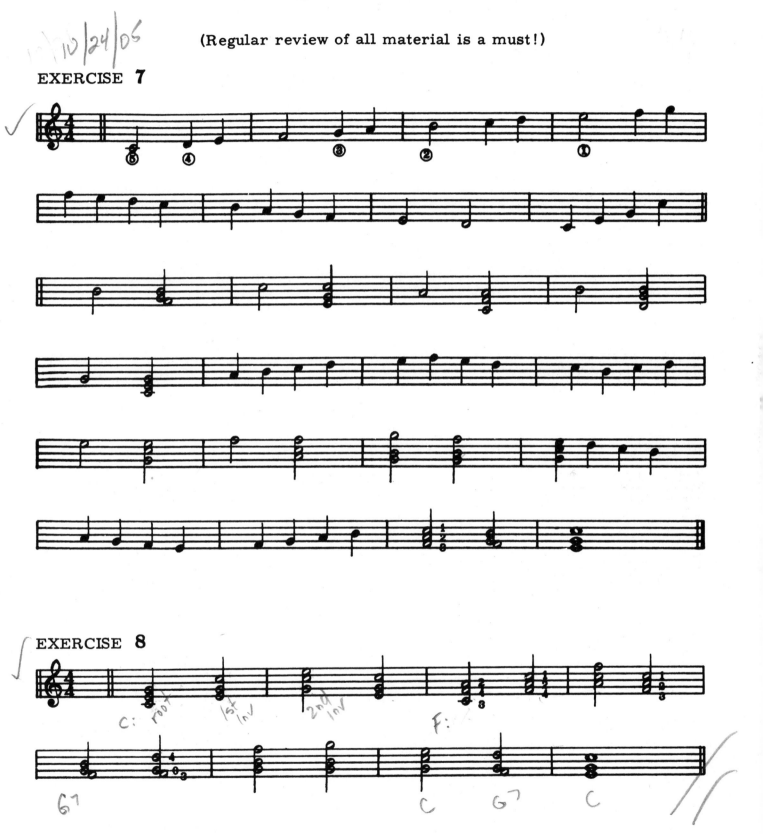

EXERCISE 8

9

One, Two, Three, Four (duet)

Tempo - Moderate 4
(speed)

Rhythm Accompaniment

(CHORD SYMBOL
- OR NAME)

STRUM AGAIN FOR EACH DIAGONAL LINE

Letters Only

10/31/06

C   F   C   G7

(*)

HOLD 2 BEATS LIKE A HALF NOTE

C   F   C   G7   C

(*) A BETTER RHYTHMIC PULSE IS PRODUCED IF YOU RELAX LEFT HAND
PRESSURE AT·THESE POINTS(٩). HOWEVER, DO NOT REMOVE FINGERS
FROM STRINGS. ALSO, IF OPEN STRINGS ARE INVOLVED, MUTE THEM
WITH THE SIDE OF THE RIGHT HAND AT THE SAME INSTANT THAT YOU
RELAX LEFT HAND PRESSURE.

"LEDGER" lines are added below or above the staff for
notes too low or too high to appear on the staff......

EXERCISE 9

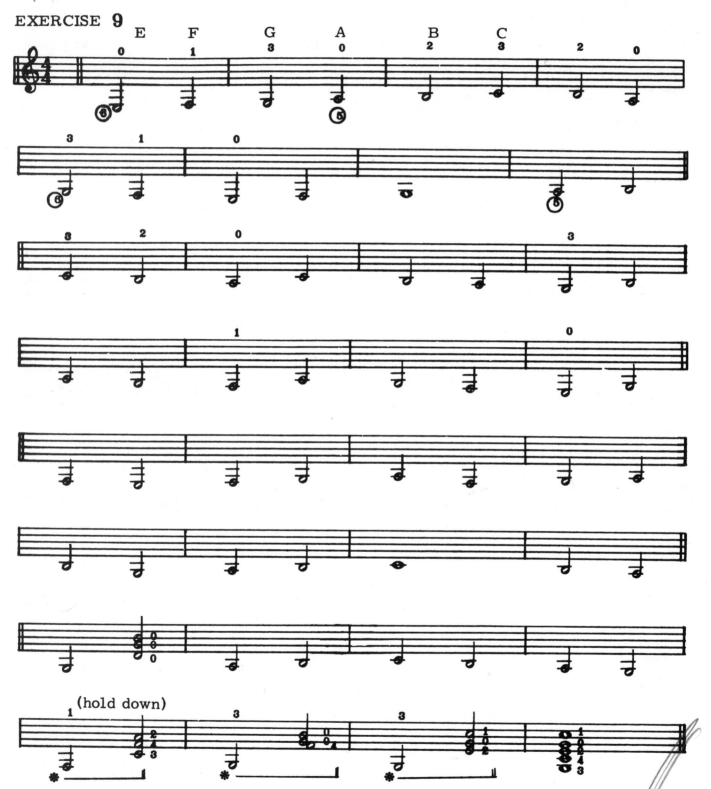

Review

Complete 1st position.. Key of C Major

EXERCISE 10

(hold down)

(let ring)   (hold down)

13

Imitation Duet

(1st Guitar)

(2nd Guitar)

Sharps and Flats

All notes that are not altered by sharps
or flats are called "NATURAL".......

SHARP (#) raises a note 1/2 tone (1 fret)   FLAT (♭) lowers a note 1/2 tone (1 fret)

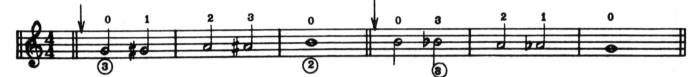

When a SHARP or FLAT appears in the KEY SIGNATURE (between
the clef sign and the time) it is used through-out the entire piece..

When a SHARP or FLAT appears in a piece that is not in the SIGNATURE, it is
called an "ACCIDENTAL", and is used only for the remainder of that measure..

...THE NEXT BAR LINE CANCELS IT OUT...

The NATURAL SIGN(♮) is used to cancel out accidentals within the same measure..
..it is also used as a "reminder" that a bar line has canceled an accidental

When the NATURAL sign is used to cancel a sharp or flat found in the key
signature, cancellation is good only for the remainder of the measure...

EXERCISE

15

12/5/05

Here We Go Again (duet)

(1st GTR)

(2nd Gtr)

"MUTE" OR DEADEN THE 5th STRING BY LIGHTLY TOUCHING IT WITH THE
SIDE OF THE 3rd FINGER SO IT WILL NOT SOUND

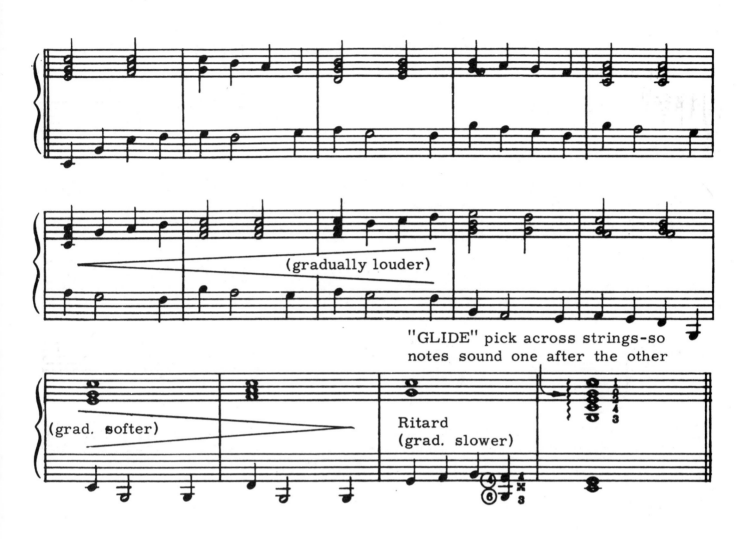

"GLIDE" pick across strings-so
notes sound one after the other

Ritard
(grad. slower)

(grad. softer)

(gradually louder)

Rhythm Accompaniment

BASS NOTES AND CHORDS

All chord symbols (names) appearing as only a letter are assumed
to be MAJOR chords. A letter followed by the numeral "7" represents
DOMINANT 7th chords. A letter followed by a small "m" are MINOR

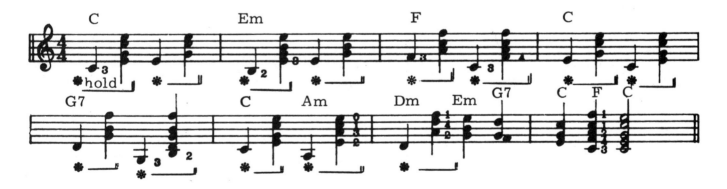

(Do not skip or "slight" any lesson material)

Eighth Notes - Counting and Picking

⊓ means pick downward   ∨ means pick upward

EXERCISE 1

count 1 & 2 & 3 & 4 &

count 1 2 & 3 4 &

EXERCISE 2

"FERMATA"
means "hold"

(Review of all material is a must)

12/19/05

EXERCISE **3**

Etude No. 1 (duet)

fine
(The end)

"Rests", "Tied Notes", "Dotted Notes"

COMMON TIME VALUES OF "RESTS" (periods of silence)

"TIED" NOTES.. When two notes are "tied" together with a curved line, only the first note is picked.. the second note is merely held and counted

"DOTTED" NOTES.. A "dot" placed after any note increases the time value of the note by one-half. Or you may say a "dot" found next to any note receives half the time value of the note itself.

This is the same example as shown above but using "tied" notes....

EXERCISE   (count aloud as you play)

Etude No. 2 (duet)

2nd GTR "TACET" (remain silent)

fine

First Solo

Solo arrangement. . . with melody AND accompaniment.

BE SURE TO HOLD ALL NOTES FOR THEIR FULL TIME VALUES

ACCOMPANIMENT CHORD IS
PLAYED ON THE 2nd BEAT

MELODY NOTE IS PICKED ON THE 1st BEAT
AND HELD WHILE CHORD IS PLAYED

Rhythm Accompaniment

CHORD DIAGRAMS

1. Vertical lines represent strings
2. Horizontal lines represent frets (see illustration, page 3)
3. Dots represent finger placement
4. Numbers indicate fingers to be used
5. Zero means open string
6. X means muted string

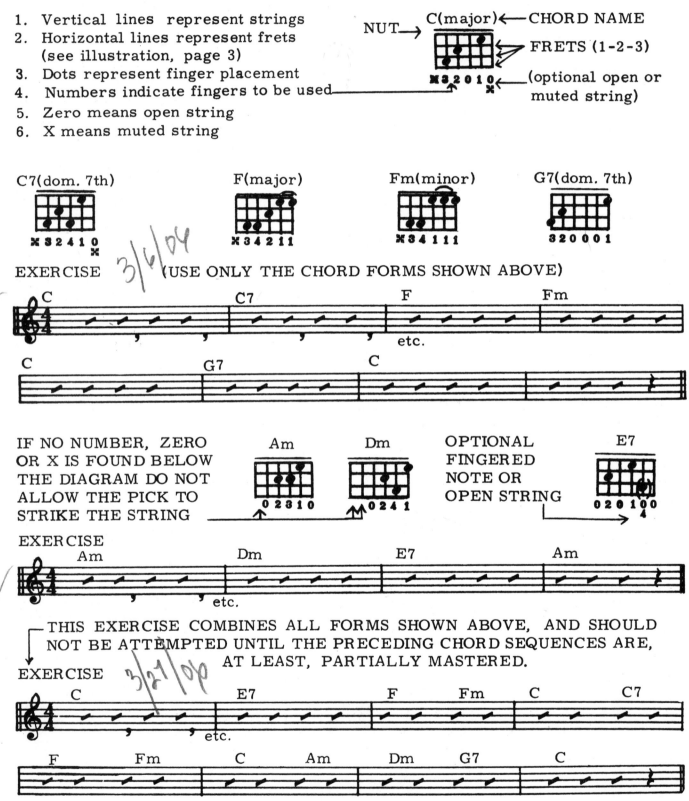

ALL CHORD FORMS MUST BE MEMORIZED

Second Solo

Solo arr. with melody above (as well as below) the chord accompaniment.

HOLD ALL NOTES FOR THEIR FULL VALUE

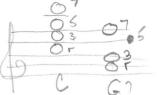

Etude No. 3 (duet)

count 1 2 3 4 &

count 1 2 3 & 4 &

1 2 & 3 4

Ritard   fine

(Review everything - Regularly)

Picking Etude No. 1

(for development of the right hand)

PREPARATION

*   1st stg, 3rd fret   **   1st stg, 5th fret
    2nd stg, 5th fret   2nd stg, 6th fret

Etude

Tempo-Moderately Slow 4

Atempo (back to Tempo)

fine

Two, Two (duet)

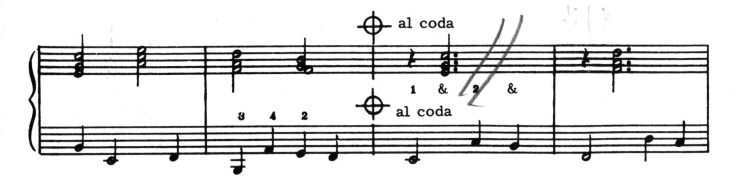

al coda

1 & 2 &

al coda

3 4 2

count 1 & 2 &

count 1 &ah 2 &

D. S. al coda

D. S. al coda

This means to play again from the (𝄋) sign to the al coda .. then skip to the coda (⊕)

coda

coda

3 4 2

1
2

1
2
0

fine

29

Key of G (1st position)

(All F's are sharped)

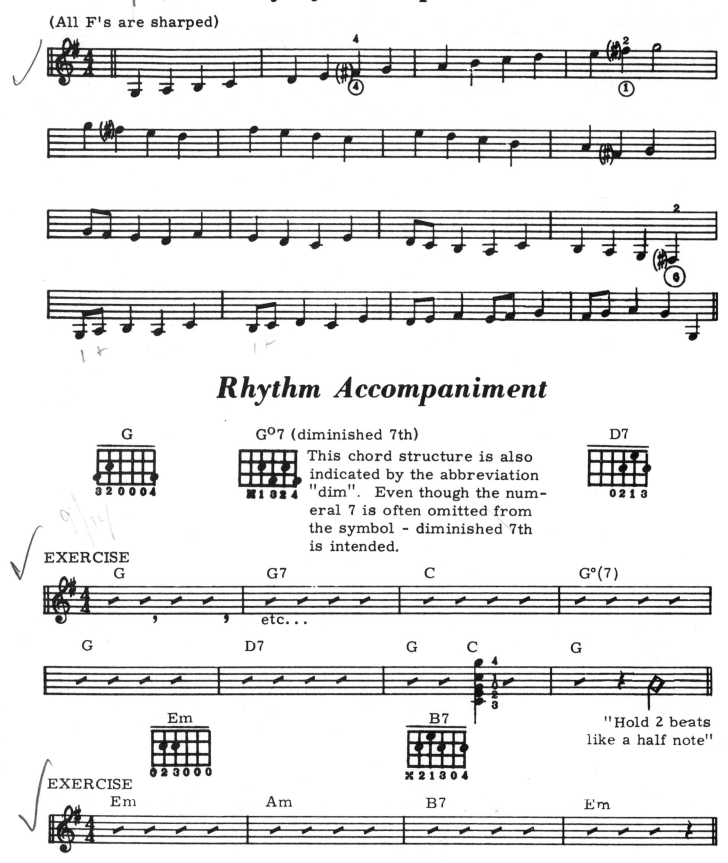

Rhythm Accompaniment

G
320004

G°7 (diminished 7th)
X1324

This chord structure is also indicated by the abbreviation "dim". Even though the numeral 7 is often omitted from the symbol - diminished 7th is intended.

D7
0213

EXERCISE

| G | G7 | C | G°(7) |

, , etc...

| G | D7 | G C | G |

"Hold 2 beats like a half note"

Em
023000

B7
X21304

EXERCISE

| Em | Am | B7 | Em |

30

Sixteenth Notes

31

Duet in G

5/1/06

fine

5/6/04

Picking Etude No. 2

FOR ALTERNATE PICKING...WHILE SKIPPING STRINGS

PAY VERY STRICT ATTENTION TO "DOWN" & "UP"
PICKING ON ALL 8th NOTE PASSAGES

REPEAT sign
(Back to Measure 1)

(hold bottom notes full value)

Repeat from preceding sign
(facing opposite direction)

(hold down top note)

fine

Another Duet in G

Key of F (1st position)

(All B's are flatted)

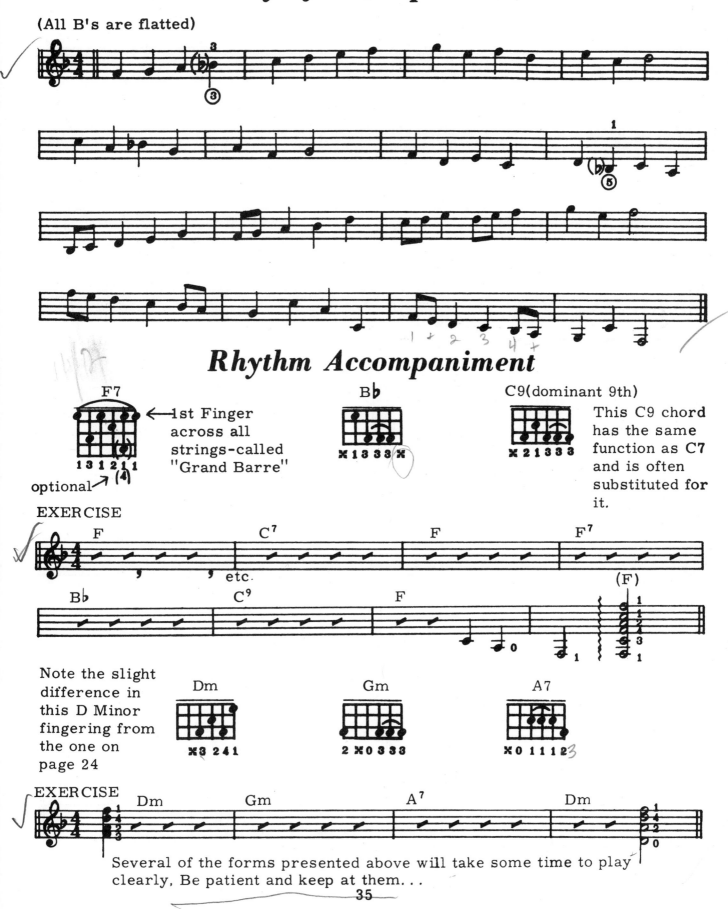

Rhythm Accompaniment

F7 — 1st Finger across all strings—called "Grand Barre"
131211
optional (4)

Bb
X 1 3 3 3 X

C9 (dominant 9th) — This C9 chord has the same function as C7 and is often substituted for it.
X 2 1 3 3 3

EXERCISE

F | C7 | F | F7
Bb | C9 | F | (F)

Note the slight difference in this D Minor fingering from the one on page 24

Dm
X3 241

Gm
2 X0 3 3 3

A7
X0 1 1 1 2 3

EXERCISE

Dm | Gm | A7 | Dm

Several of the forms presented above will take some time to play clearly, Be patient and keep at them...

Duet in F

The Triplet

There are two ways to pick consecutive sets of Triplets.
Practice the entire exercise thoroughly, using first the
picking marked TYPE 1... then practice using TYPE 2..

REVIEW ALL MATERIAL

37

Waltz in F (solo)

(A "Waltz" has 3 beats per measure)

notes appearing before the beginning
measure are called "PICK-UPS"

count 2 3 1 2 3 etc..

Rallentando (slow down)   Atempo (back in tempo)

upper notes

12/14 uppernotes

Ritard - poco a poco (little by little)

fine

Key of A Minor

(Relative to C Major)

The sixth "degree" or note of any major scale is the "tonic" or 1st note, of its "RELATIVE MINOR KEY". The major and relative minor key signatures are the same. There are 3 different scales in each minor key...

A-NATURAL MINOR (All notes exactly the same as its relative, C Major)

A-HARMONIC MINOR (The 7th degree, counting up from A, is raised 1/2 step)

A-MELODIC MINOR
(The 6th and 7th degrees are raised ASCENDING - but, return to normal descending)

Rhythm Accompaniment

- We now begin to observe that many chords have more than one fingering. The choice of which one to use generally depends upon the chord fingerings that immediately preceed and/or follow. In the following exercise use the large diagrams OR the smaller optional fingerings in sequence - DO NOT MIX THEM....

EXERCISE

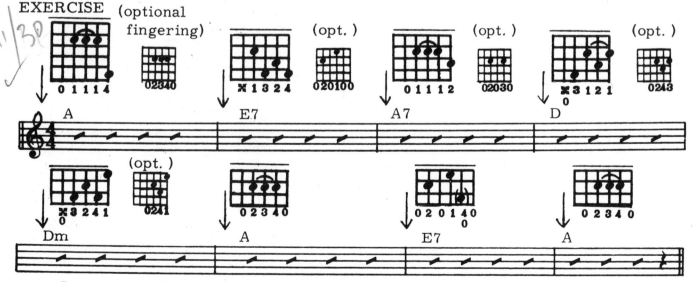

Smooth, melodic rhythm accompaniment depends on the number of chord forms mastered.

Pretty Pickin' (*duet*)

For alternate picking. . . while skipping strings

CHORD PREPARATION

slowly

fine

1/18/01

Duet

Moderate Waltz Tempo

(All notes under the curved line must be kept ringing)

CRESCENDO
(get louder)

DIMINUENDO
(get softer)

CRESC.

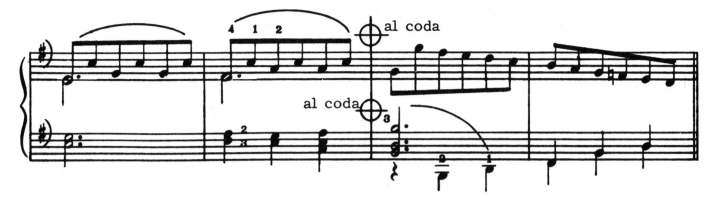

al coda

al coda

D. C.
al coda

DIM.

D. C.
al coda

(Repeat from
the beginning
to the coda)

coda

coda

fine

Dotted Eighth and Sixteenth

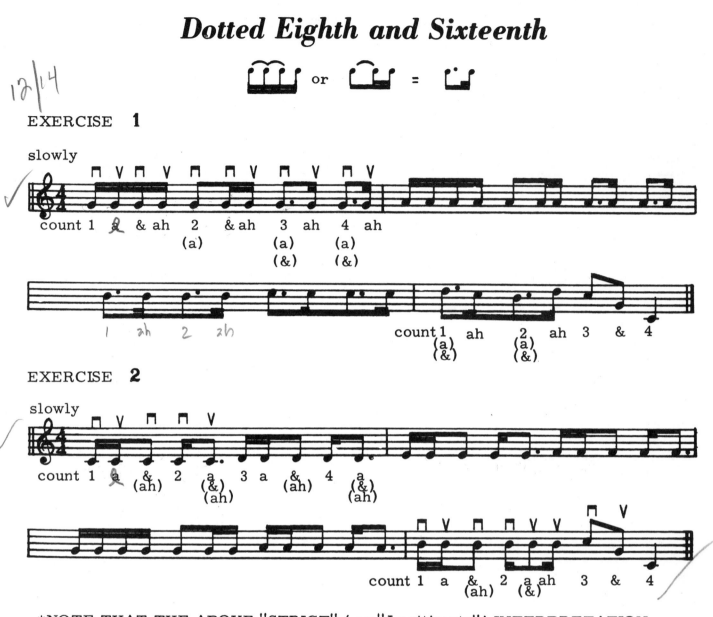

EXERCISE 1

slowly

count 1 a & ah 2 & ah 3 ah 4 ah
(a) (a) (a)
(&) (&)

1 ah 2 ah

count 1 ah 2 ah 3 & 4
(a) (a)
(&) (&)

EXERCISE 2

slowly

count 1 a & 2 a 3 a & 4 a
(ah) (&) (ah) (&)
(ah) (ah) (ah)

count 1 a & 2 a ah 3 & 4
(ah) (&)

*NOTE THAT THE ABOVE "STRICT" (or "Legitimate") INTERPRETATION
OF DOTTED 8th AND 16th NOTES PRODUCES A RATHER "JERKY" RHYTHM..
IN "POP" MUSIC (OR JAZZ) THEY ARE PLAYED MORE "LEGATO" (smoothly,
in a flowing manner). THIS IS DONE BY TREATING THEM AS TRIPLETS...

Example : or =

EXERCISE 3

slowly

count 1 & ah 2 & ah 3 & ah 4 ah
(&) (&)

(be sure to keep the "3" feeling)

42

Key of E Minor

(Relative to G Major)

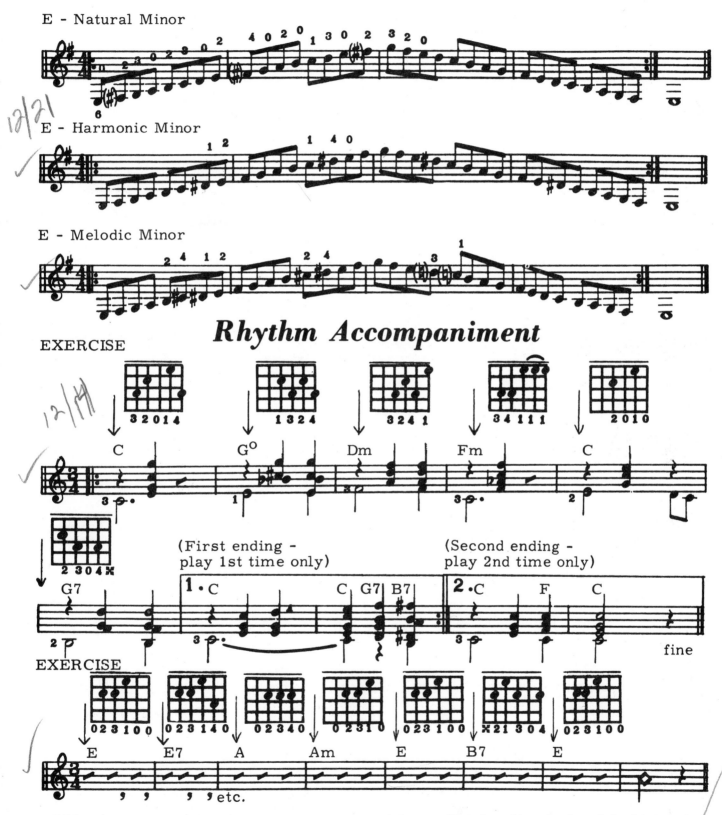

Rhythm Accompaniment

(First ending –
play 1st time only)

(Second ending –
play 2nd time only)

fine

(Observe: in waltz time chords are muted immediately after 2nd and 3rd beats)

Take Your Pick (*duet*)

(For alternate picking. . While skipping strings)

Chord Preparation

slowly

fine

DUET

Moderately Slow

Rhythm Accompaniment
THE PRINCIPLE OF MOVABLE CHORD FORMS

Moving up the fingerboard (in pitch) - all NATURAL notes are two frets apart, except E to F, and B to C... they are one fret apart.
EXAMPLE(1st or 6th stg)

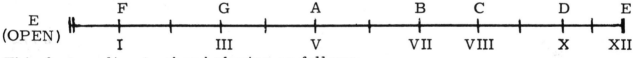

This fact applies to chord playing as follows:

1.) If you play F major, F minor and F^7 on the 1st fret then (using the same fingering) G major, G minor and G^7 will be on the 3rd fret, or two frets above F. Moving still higher A maj, A min and A^7 will be on the fifth fret, B maj, B min, B^7 on the seventh fret and C maj, C min, C^7 will be on the eighth - ONE fret up from B.

2.) ALL MOVABLE forms will have NO OPEN STRINGS.

3.) Sharps and flats alter chord positions by one fret, the same as single notes.

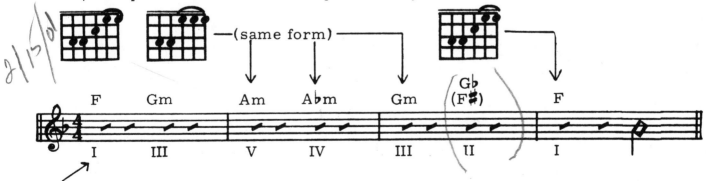

(The Roman numerals (called Position Marks) indicate the frets on which the 1st finger plays)

ON THE FOLLOWING PAGES ALL NEW CHORD FORMS WILL BE MOVABLE

Chromatic Scale (1st position)

The Chromatic Scale is made up of "semi-tones" (half steps)

Speed Studies

Play the follwoing 8th note patterns at an even speed, slowly at first, and very gradually (over a period of time) increase the tempo. MEMORIZE the PATTERNS, and practice each one in all keys. Always start on the "Tonic" (1st note) of each scale and "transpose" the rest of the notes by following the pattern. (Write it out if necessary)

Pattern 1

Pattern 2

Pattern 3

(1st pos. F and G scales contain two octaves - play all patterns in BOTH octaves)

46

Key of D Minor
(Relative to F Major)

Rhythm Accompaniment

(This is the same chord sequence but TRANSPOSED
to a different key - watch the position marks)

Note: The augmented chord can actually be named from any note within the form.
(Example C+ = E+ = G#+ or Ab+) Augmented chords repeat themselves every 5th
fret.

Endurance Etude

PICKING ETUDE #3

(HOLD 4th FINGER DOWN THRU-OUT)

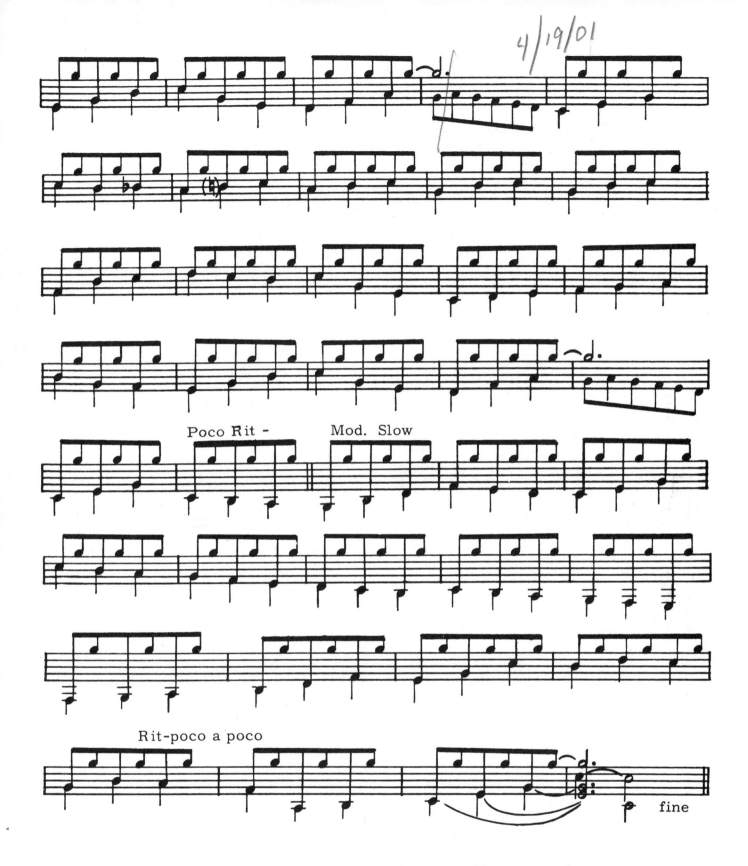

Be sure to observe the tempo changes. Also, vary the "DYNAMICS" (degrees of volume, loud and soft) to make the music more interesting to listen to.

5/10/01

Key of Bb (1st position)

(All B's and E's are flatted)

fine

WHEN A KEY SIGNATURE HAS TWO OR MORE FLATS-THE NAME
OF THE NEXT TO LAST FLAT IS THE NAME OF THE KEY

Rhythm Accompaniment

Fm

Bbm

Mute 5th stg
with tip of
first finger
Mute 6th by
touching with
the thumb →

G°
also called
G dim
(see pg 30)

4/9/01

EXERCISE

count 1 2 and 3 4

Note: The diminished chord can actually be named from any note in the form. (Ex. G° = Bb° = C#° or Db° = E°) Diminished chords repeat themselves every 4th fret.

EXERCISE (This is the same chord sequence but TRANSPOSED to a different key - watch the position marks)

50

Duet in Bb

5/3 chords

Mod. Slow Tempo

(Finger complete chord form
Do not strum top string)

Bb F7

1. 2.

F7 Bb Bb D7

Gm D7 Gm C7 F

C7 F7 Bb F7

F7 Bb fine

51

Reverse Alternate Picking Study

PAY VERY STRICT ATTENTION TO PICKING AS INDICATED...

5/10

(hold down bottom note)

REVIEW ALL MATERIAL

Key of D (1st position)

(All F's and C's are sharped)

IN ANY SHARP SIGNATURE THE FIRST NOTE ABOVE
THE LAST SHARP IS THE NAME OF THE KEY

Duet in D

count (1 2) 3 4 &   1 & 2 & 3 (4   1) & 2 & 3 (4)

Dot over a note means staccato

Play like this.   II   fine

Dynamic Etude (duet)

ETUDE #4

Moderato

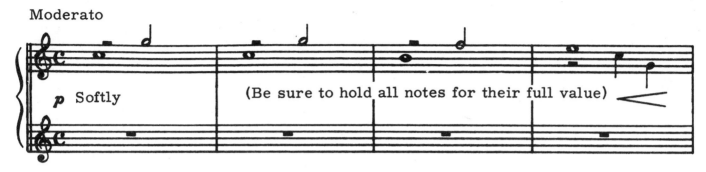

p Softly (Be sure to hold all notes for their full value)

mp (moderately soft)

mf Moderately loud

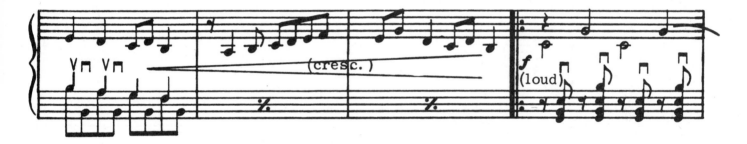

Key of A (1st position)

DUET IN A

ALL F's, C's and G's are sharped

Rhythm Accompaniment

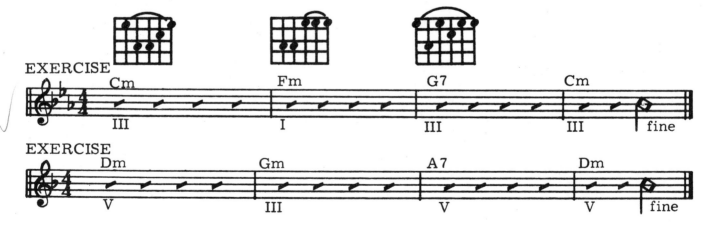

Key of Eb (1st position)

(All B's, E's and A's are flatted)

Duet in Eb

Mod. 4 (swing feeling) (Remember the flats - count the time carefully)

C flat - same as B♮
-2nd stg open or 4th
finger - 3rd stg.

fine

57

Movable Chord Forms

(A COMPILATION OF ALL MOVABLE FORMS PRESENTED IN SECTION I)

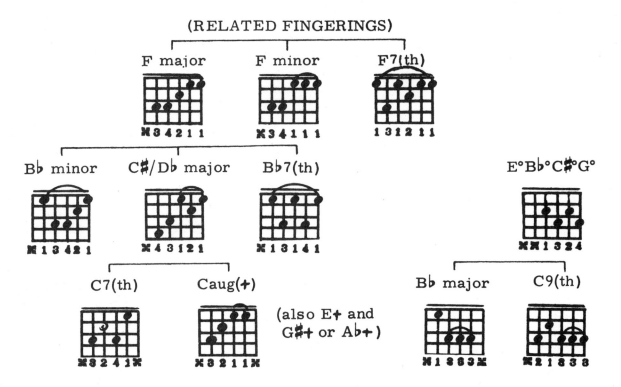

With these eleven forms you are now able to play the accompaniment to any song in any key providing -1) That you understand the principle of movable chord forms discussed on pg. 45, -2) That you observe the following chart...

CHORD SIMPLIFICATION AND SUBSTITUTION CHART

MAJOR	C6	Cmaj7	Cmaj9	C^9_6	$Cmaj^9_7$	USE:	C major
DOMINANT 7th **DOM 7-ALTERED 9th**	C9 C7(-9) C7(+9)	C13 C7(b9) C7(#9)	C9(11+) C13(-9) C13(+9)	C11+ C13(b9) etc.	———— ———— ————	USE:	— C7 — C7 or G dim {build dim chord — C7 (or G°) {on 5th note above C
DOM 7-ALTERED 5th **DOM 7-ALTERED 5, 9**	C7+ C7(-5) $C7^{-9}_{+5}$	C7(+5) C7(b5) $C7^{+9}_{+5}$	Caug7 C9(-5) $C7^{+9}_{-5}$	C9+ etc... $C7^{-9}_{-5}$	C9(+5) C+9 $C7^{-5}_{+5}$ —— ————	USE:	C+ — C+ or Gb+ {build substitute — C+ or Gb7 {chord on flatted {5th above C
DOM 7-SUS 4	C7(sus4)	C7(susF)	C9(sus4)	C9(susF)	C11	USE:	G minor 5th note above C
MINOR	Cm6	Cm^9_6				USE:	C minor
MINOR 7th	Cm7	Cm9	Cm11			USE:	Cm
MIN-WITH MAJ 7	Cm(♮7)	Cm(#7)	Cm(maj7)			USE:	G+(5th above C) or Cm
MIN 7-ALTERED 5th	Cm7(-5)	Cm7(b5)				USE:	Ebm {built on minor, (or {lowered)3rd above C

Of course having only eleven chord forms at your command will cause you to move up and down the fingerboard much more than is desirable for good rhythm playing.. The more forms you know - the less distance you have to travel, and the more melodic your rhythm playing can become...

Picking - A Different Technique

THE PRINCIPLE IS TO ATTACK EACH NEW STRING WITH A DOWN STROKE

This technique is older than alternate picking, and less emphasis is placed on it today. However it is one more step in right hand control - and when mastered it is very fast in ascending passages.

An example of this technique in use can be found on page 48, measure twenty of the Endurance Etude. This type of picking will be suggested on the following pages from time to time BUT only in certain situations; (arpeggios - whole tone scales, etc.) and only IN ADDITION TO ALTERNATE PICKING. It will be up to the student to gradually master and (whenever practical) add this style to his over-all right hand technique. However: THE MOST CONCENTRATED EFFORT MUST STILL BE PLACED ON ALTERNATE PICKING.

* (>) Accent mark - strike more sharply

SECTION TWO
Position Playing

POSITION IS DETERMINED BY THE FRET ON WHICH THE FIRST FINGER PLAYS
AND THIS IS INDICATED BY A ROMAN NUMERAL. A POSITION ON THE FINGER-
BOARD (STRICTLY SPEAKING) OCCUPIES FOUR ADJACENT FRETS. SOME
SCALES HAVE ONE OR MORE NOTES THAT FALL OUTSIDE THIS FOUR FRET
AREA AND THESE NOTES ARE TO BE PLAYED BY REACHING OUT WITH THE
1st OR 4th FINGER WITHOUT SHIFTING THE ENTIRE HAND..i.e. FINGER
STRETCH OR F.S. ..WHEN THE OUT OF POSITION NOTE IS A SCALE TONE
THE F.S. IS DETERMINED BY THE FINGERING TYPE..(FINGERING TYPE
I = 1st FINGER STRETCH, TYPE IV = 4th F.S.) WHEN THE OUT OF POSITION
NOTE IS NOT A SCALE TONE AND MOVING UPWARD USE F.S. 1, AND MOV-
ING DOWNWARD F.S. 4...REGARDLESS OF FINGERING TYPE......(ALL
SCALE FINGERINGS INTRODUCED FROM THIS POINT ON WILL NOT USE ANY
OPEN STRINGS, AND THEREFORE THEY ARE MOVABLE, IN THE SAME MAN-
NER AS THE CHORD FORMS PRESENTED EARLIER..SEE P. 45)

Major Scales

C MAJOR (FINGERING TYPE 1) (2nd Position)

60

*   When an out of position note is immediately preceeded or followed by a note played with the same finger that would normally make the stretch, reverse the usual F.S. procedure...always move back into a position from an F.S.--never away from it.

EIGHTH NOTE STUDY

ARPEGGIO STUDY   BROKEN CHORDS

(Practice picking as indicated--and also with alternate ⊓V)

**   When two consecutive notes are played with the same finger on adjacent strings - "roll" the finger tip from one string to the next-do not lift the finger from the string....

Chord Etude No. 1

Practice slowly and evenly "connecting" the chords so they "flow" from one to the next with no silences between them . . . observe fingering and position marks!

62

Etude No. 5

(Remember - All natural notes on the guitar are 2 frets apart, except E to F and B to C)

Reading Studies

DO NOT PRACTICE these two pages...just READ them, but not more than twice thru-during any single practice session... Do not play them on two consecutive days... Do not go back over any particular section because of a wrong note ... DO KEEP AN EVEN TEMPO and play the proper time values ... By obeying these rules the "Reading Studies" will never be memorized ... A little later on it is recommended that you use this procedure with a variety of material as this is the only way for a guitarist to achieve and maintain any proficiency in reading. (Even when working steady we are not reading every day - so "scare yourself in the privacy of your practice sessions" . . . .

C MAJOR (FINGERING TYPE 1)

fine

(If unusual difficulty is encountered reading these pages - go back to Page 60 and start again.)

Ballad (duet)

(* Position mark in parenthesis represents placement of 2nd finger as 1st finger is not used.)

66

Rit-- *(III) (II) fine
(III) (II)

Movable Chord Forms

(RHYTHM ACCOMPANIMENT, PART TWO)

The most difficult part of learning to play chords on the guitar is that of getting the fingers to fall instantly, and without conscious effort, in the proper arrangement on the fingerboard. This is mainly a physical problem and a certain amount of practice time seems to be the only solution.

However, I have found that by presenting new chord forms to a student in a certain order (a sequence of related fingerings) it seems to lessen the time normally required for him to perform them.

Therefore, the following chord forms are presented in a particular order. We will use three of the previously learned fingerings as basic forms..... We will alter these forms by moving, or removing one or more fingers..... In this way each new fingering is directly related to the one(s) preceding it.....

So... each of the basic forms and each derivative is a preparation for another new chord form.

No specific letter names are given- only the chord type and the string on which the root is found.

***Memorize the fingering for all chord structures in the order of their appearance .....Do not skip around. Do not change the fingering of any form, even if you already play it but in a different way. It will appear later on with "your" fingering..but related to a new set of forms. Practice all chord forms chromatically up and down the fingerboard observing root (chord) names.

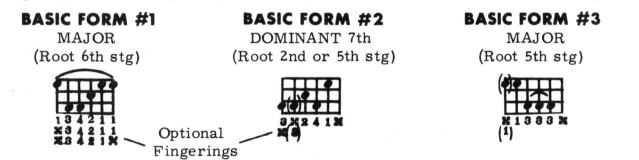

BASIC FORM #1
MAJOR
(Root 6th stg)

BASIC FORM #2
DOMINANT 7th
(Root 2nd or 5th stg)

BASIC FORM #3
MAJOR
(Root 5th stg)

Optional Fingerings

The dot in parenthesis (•) means that altho-the note belongs to the chord it need not sound..... and in many cases sounds better without it.

Chord Forms

Shown below is Basic Form #1 and seven derivative fingerings. When the basic form has been mastered the performance of the derivatives is relatively easy to accomplish. MEMORIZE the type of chord (maj., min., etc.) each form produces and the string on which the root (or name) is found. All optional fingerings should eventually be learned, but at first concentrate on the one appearing directly below the diagram... it is the preferred one.

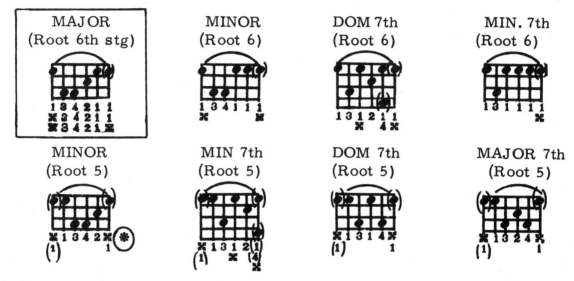

A Word about notation:

1. When a chord is indicated by just a letter it is **major**.
2. When it is a letter followed by a 7, it is a dominant 7th chord.
3. Minor is indicated by min., m, or a dash (-)
4. Major 7th is Gmaj7, Gma7, or sometimes GM7

EXERCISE   (Using only the forms shown above... watch the position marks!)

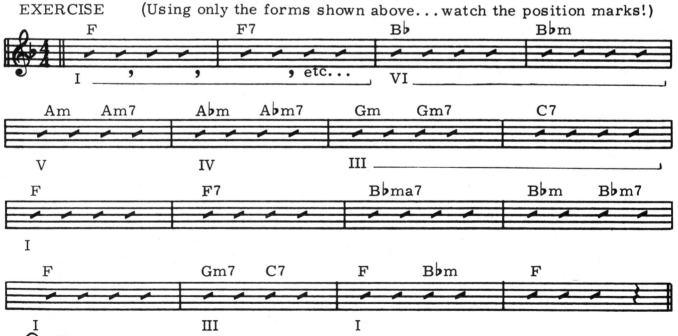

⊛ The 1st string is not very effective in rhythm playing, and even when it is pressed down with a "barre" it is usually best to omit it by making the pick travel in an arc across the strings, passing above it

Rhythm Accompaniment - Right Hand Technique

To most beginners, "strumming" chords (by pushing the pick across the stgs so they sound one after the other) is easy and natural.

However, striking the chords so that the sound fits with a modern rhythm section is quite another thing, and requires considerable practice and know-how.

First, by using a combination rotary forearm, and loose wrist motion (snap the wrist as if "flecking" something from the back of your hand) you produce an "explosive" attack (where all notes seem to sound simultaneously).

Secondly, the placement of "pressure release points" (❡) and accents determine the type of beat produced. (Much more about all this later...)

Picking Etude No. 4
(OBSERVE FINGERING)

(* "GRACE NOTE" to be played slightly before the top note G which falls on the 4th beat.)

F MAJOR (FINGERING TYPE 1A)
2ND POSITION

The F Major scale shown above is in the 2nd position even tho the first finger plays the 1st fret on three strings. This is because these three scale tones require stretches by the first finger. The basic four fret position is never numbered from a stretch ...

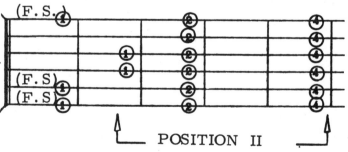

EIGHTH NOTE STUDY

ARPEGGIO STUDY

(Also practice arpeggios with alt. ⊓ V picking, which is generally the most practical.)

Chord Forms

BASIC FORM #2 DOM 7th (Root 5 or 2)	AUGMENTED(+) (Root any stg.)	AUG. (add 9) (Root 5)	DOM 7th(+5) (Root 4)

written E7(+5)   E7+
E+7   E7aug

EXERCISE   (Using the above forms plus some of the preceding ones.)

(add 9)

F	E7	Eb7	D7 D+ D+
I	V	IV	III

G7 G+ G7(+5) C7	F Bb7	F
III IV III I		

****Transpose and write out all rhythm exercises one or more keys higher and practice.

71

Chord Etude No. 2

These chord exercises are very important and should be
reviewed <u>regularly</u> as they serve many purposes, such as
physical development of the left hand.. fingering relation-
ship between chord structures, and eventual "chord picture"
recognition......

Another Duet in F

F.S.

(Hold down all notes under curved lines)

(also with alt. ⊓V)

fine

(Regular review is a must!)

Reading Studies

Do not "practice" these Reading Studies, do not
play on two consecutive days. (See top Page 64).

F MAJOR (FINGERING TYPE 1A)

F.S.

fine

(F.S. - Stretch the finger - Don't move the entire hand)

Play it Pretty (duet)

(*) A temporary change to position III at this point will simplify the
fingering of this passage, and eliminate the necessity of the open E
(preceeding the high B♭).

Chord Forms

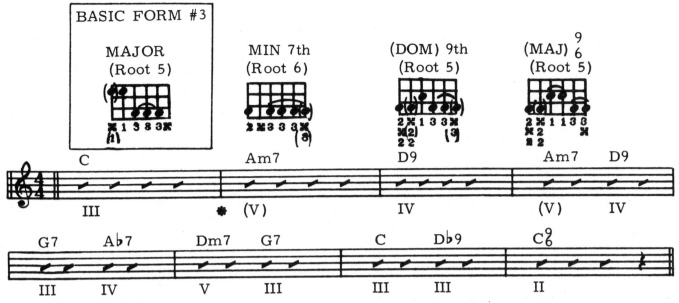

* When a pos. mark is found in parentheses it means the 1st finger is
omitted from the form...and position is determined by the lowest
numbered finger used.

Triplet Study

(Practice using both types of picking - See Page 37)

Speed Study - fingering type 1

Maintain an EVEN TEMPO. --
Play no faster than perfect
co-ordination in both hands will
allow. --An increase in speed
will come gradually...

Speed Study - fingering type 1A

Practice all speed studies as written and as ♩♩ . Also play them with, and without repeats...

(For additional technique building patterns, see Page 46).

G Major - fingering type 2 (2nd position)

EIGHTH NOTE STUDY

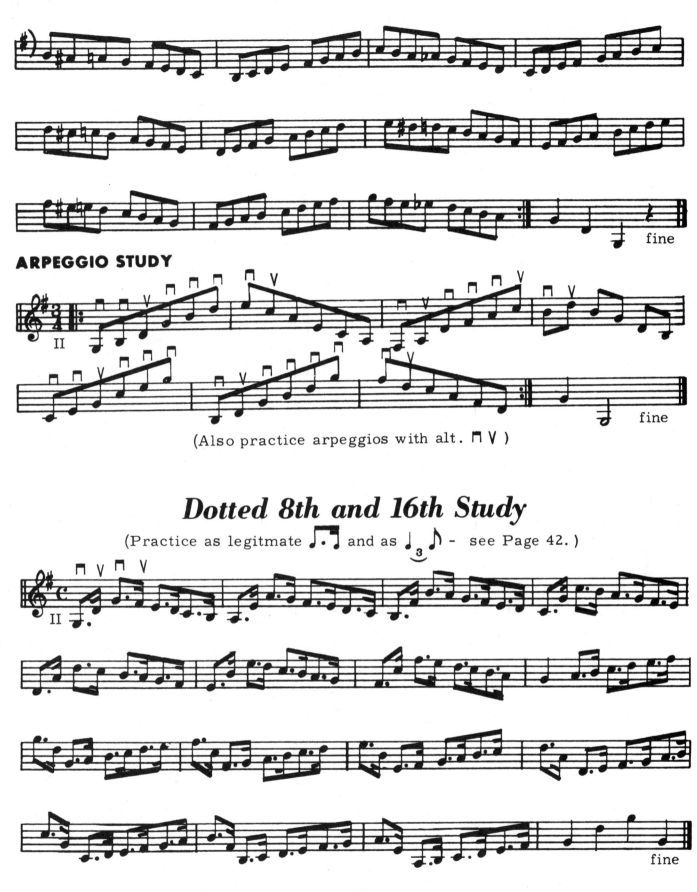

ARPEGGIO STUDY

(Also practice arpeggios with alt. ⊓ V)

Dotted 8th and 16th Study

(Practice as legitmate ♪. ♪ and as ♩ ♪ - see Page 42.)

(When 2 consecutive notes on adjacent stgs. require the same finger - roll fingertip - don't lift.)

81

Waltz for Two (duet)

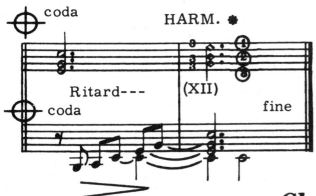

coda

HARM. ✱

Ritard--- coda

(XII)

fine

*HARMONIC... lay the 3rd finger lightly on the strings directly over the 12th fret..sharply strike the strings indicated, removing the 3rd finger at almost the same instant. The resulting sound is in the same octave as notated. (One octave above what you would expect to hear, as the guitar sounds one octave below the written note.) These "natural" harmonics (from open strings) are also possible on other frets... the most practical being the 7th and 5th...

Chord Forms

(From this dom7th we derive the dim7)

(7th)

Diminished 7th (°) (Root any stg)

M 2 3 1 4 X

(From this min. we derive the maj7)

(min.)

Maj 7th (Root 6)

1 X 3 4 2 M

A word about notation.. diminished 7th chords are indicated by; Gdim, G°......(the 7th is assumed).

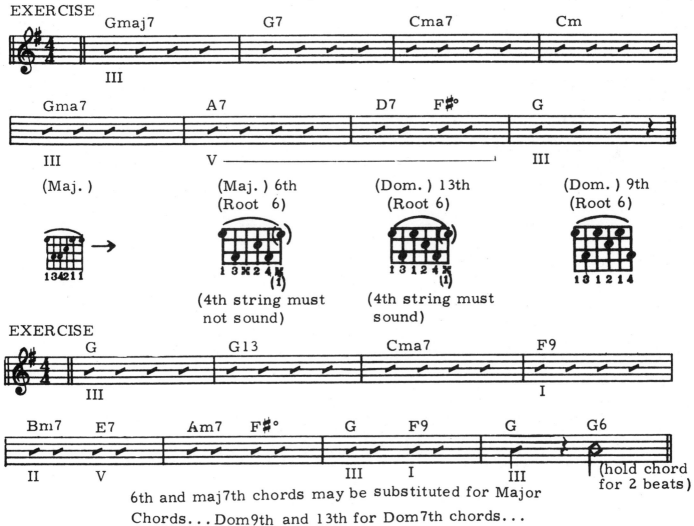

(Maj.)

134211

(Maj.) 6th (Root 6)

1 3 X 2 4 M

(1)

(4th string must not sound)

(Dom.) 13th (Root 6)

1 3 1 2 4 X

(1)

(4th string must sound)

(Dom.) 9th (Root 6)

1 3 1 2 1 4

6th and maj7th chords may be substituted for Major Chords...Dom9th and 13th for Dom7th chords...

Reading Studies

Do not "practice" Reading Studies - just read them.

G MAJOR (FINGERING TYPE 2)

(Continue on - without stopping - same tempo - but in waltz time)

Speed not coming? Left hand accuracy not consistant? ... Play any scale
very slowly...watch your left hand...force your fingers to remain poised
over the fingerboard always in readiness...don't let them move too far
away from the strings when not in use-concentrate on this...

Blues in G (duet)

.....The 1st guitar part of this duet is often played using the "muffled effect."
This sound is produced by laying the right hand lightly along the top of the bridge.
All strings being played must be kept covered. As this somewhat inhibits picking,
the part should first be thoroughly practiced without the muffled effect (or "open").

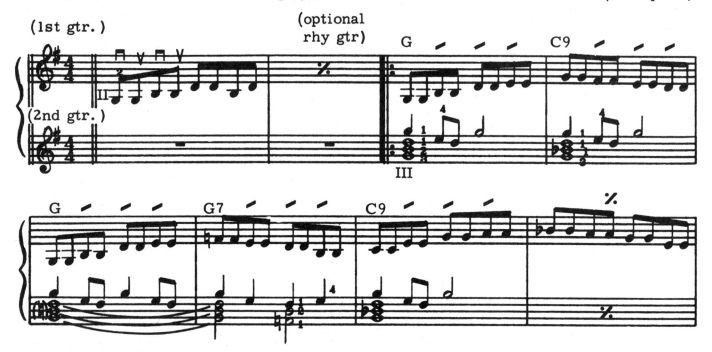

(Accent mark = strike sharply)

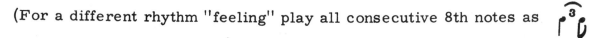

(For a different rhythm "feeling" play all consecutive 8th notes as   )

Chord Etude No. 3

Observe position marks and fingerings...as
they will make possible a smooth performance.

When moving from chord to chord the best fingering is usually the one that
involves the least motion in the left hand... Leaving one finger free for
possible melodic additions is also an important factor.

Rhythm Accompaniment - Right Hand Technique

SYMBOLS: ⊓ = down stroke... V = up stroke... (ʼ) = release finger pressure (of left hand immediately AFTER chord sounds - do not remove fingers from stgs)... ⊓ˣ = strike deadened strings (fingers in formation on stgs, but no pressure)... > = accent, strike sharply, with more force... (memorize these symbols).

A Basic Latin Beat... which will work with the cha-cha, Beguine, Samba and others...

Picking Etude No. 5

(Hold down 4th finger thru-out)

(REVIEW-REVIEW!)

88

Short and Sweet (duet)

D MAJOR - FINGERING TYPE 3 (2nd Position)

EIGHTH NOTE STUDY

ARPEGGIO STUDY

(Also practice Arpeggios with alt. ⊓ V)

Chord Forms

(7th)

(Dom.)7th(sus. 4)
(Root 6)

(7th)

(7th sus. 4)

Min. 7th
(Root 2 or 5)

Min. 7th(♭5)
(Root 2)

written Cm7 ♭5
Cm7 -5
Cm7 5♭

EXERCISE

Cma7　　G7(sus4) G7　　Em7　Em7(♭5)　A7(sus4) A7

Dm7　Dm7(-5)　G7(susC) G7　　Cma7　D♭9　C$^9_6$

The sus. 4 refers to the 4th scale degree of the chord so named... The note name (for the 4th) is also used..i.e. G7susC. Sus 4 may also be called (natural) 11th. The root is on the same string as the sus 4 form. For example in the above exercise you may substitute symbols "G11" and "A11" for sus 4.

Melodic Rhythm Study No. 1
OPTIONAL DUET WITH RHYTHM GUITAR

Be sure to COUNT the rhythm until you can "feel" the phrase. Eventually you will be able to recognize (and "feel") entire groups of syncopated notes. In the beginning you should pick DOWN for notes falling on the beat, and UP for those counted "and". This is a definite aid in learning to read these "off beat" rhythms. Later on (when syncopation is no longer a problem) you will vary your picking for the purpose of phrasing and accents.

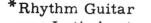

*Rhythm Guitar
use Latin beat

(* Rhy. Gtr. ⊓ V ⊓ V ⊓ V ⊓ V   or   ⊓ V ⊓ V ⊓ V ⊓ V   ...and remember

substitutions possible on (dom)7th and Maj chords.)

92

Chord Etude No. 4

(Be sure to hold all notes for their full value)

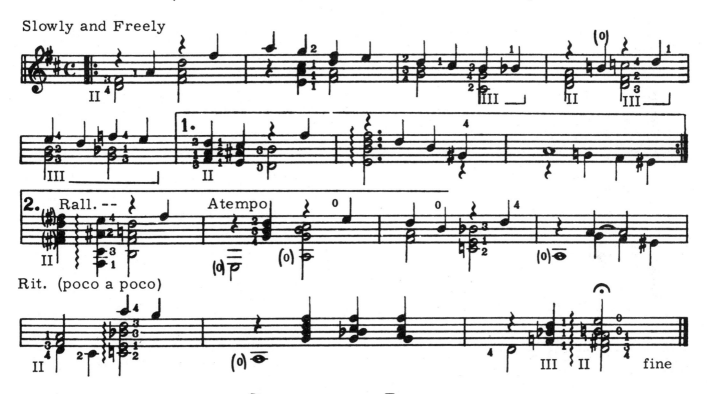

Staccato - Legato

A DOT • above or below a note
means "staccato" or short.

A LINE — above or below a note
means "legato" or long.

Reading Studies

FOR READING ONLY

D MAJOR (FINGERING TYPE 3)

Reading music is a combination of instant note (and finger) recognition and that of playing the "sound" that you "see" on the music...(along with the relative time durations of the notes of course)...Now try this--play the tonic chord of these Reading Studies (to get your "ear" in the proper key)...then try to sing the music to yourself as you play it...If your fingers have been over the fingering type enough times they will automatically play whatever notes (sound patterns) you mentally "hear" on the page...This will take a great deal of time to master...but keep after it--it's worth it...

Dee - Oo - Ett (duet)

Chord Forms

The fingering will be given as shown here whenever 2 forms are possible in the same position... and also as an occasional reminder...

EXERCISE (Latin beat--be sure to release pressure where indicated).

(The min 6th form shown above may also be called min 7th ♭5...root 5th stg.)

Speed Study - fingering type 2

Maintain an EVEN TEMPO. --Play
no faster than perfect co-ordination
in both hands will allow. An increase
in speed will come gradually....

Speed Study - fingering type 3

Practice all speed studies as
written and as ♫ . Also play
them with, and without repeats...

(For additional technique building patterns, see Page 46)

A Major - Fingering Type 4 (2nd position)

EIGHTH NOTE STUDY

ARPEGGIO STUDY

(Also practice arpeggios with alt. ⊓ V)

Chord Etude No. 5

Reading Studies

A MAJOR - FINGERING TYPE 4

Tres Sharp (duet)

16th Note Study

(Count carefully, see Page 31)

Chord Forms

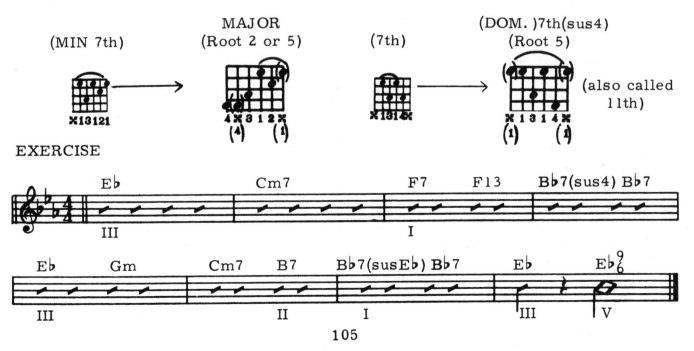

105

Speed Study - fingering type 4·

As before-keep an even tempo-play as written and as ♩.♪ -with, and without repeats.....

(For additional technique building patterns see Page 46)

Chord Forms

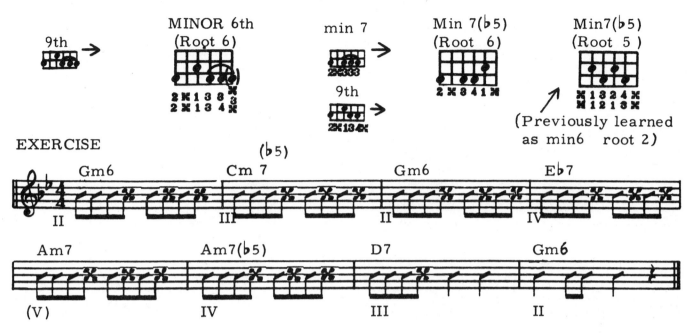

As the min 6th and min7(♭5) forms tend to get confusing, study the following exercises paying careful attention to the position marks.....Play rhythm straight 4 (as written) and also practice using Latin beat...Experiment with various "pressure release" points to vary the accents.

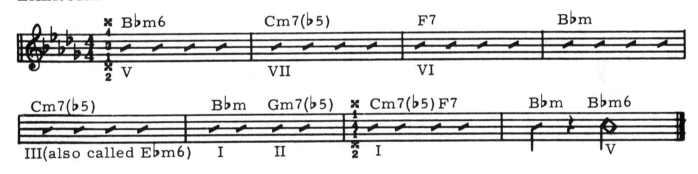

(Transpose and write out all rhythm exercises one or more keys higher and practice)

2nd Position Review

(Employing the five preceeding Maj. scales in pos. II)

When played as a duet: 1.) Melody guitar play as written-rhythm guitar play Latin beat... 2.) Melody guitar play consecutive 8th notes as ♪⁸♪ -rhythm guitar play straight 4.....

FINGERING TYPE 1

Chord Forms

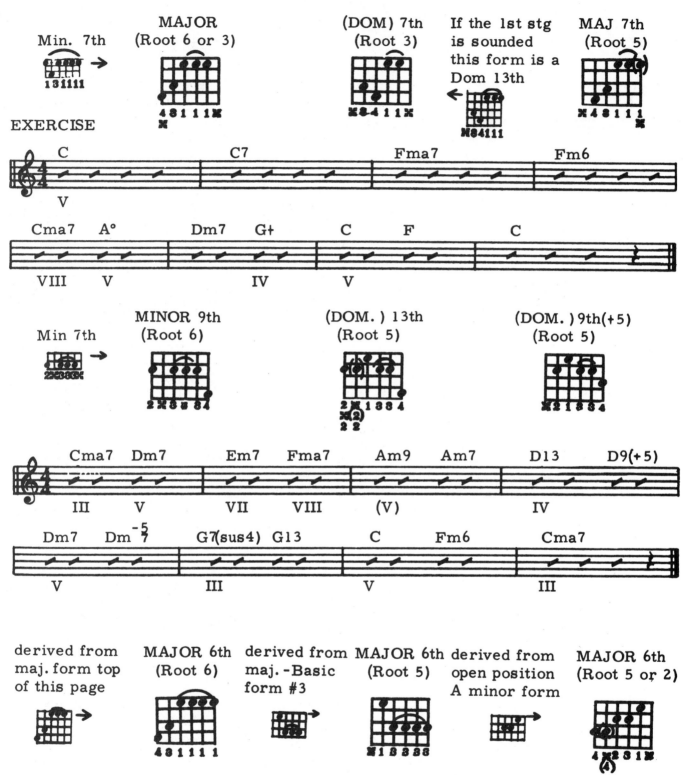

(The third major 6th form shown here is, by far, the most valuable--as it does not use the first string, and therefore has a better rhythm sound.)

Quarter Note Triplets

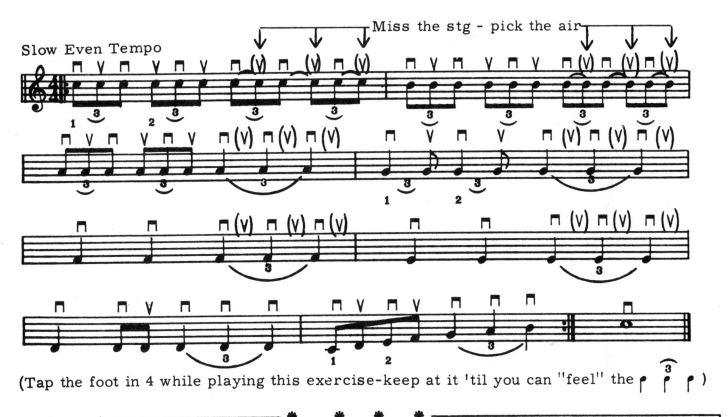

Quarter note triplets are very difficult to count.....the most practical approach is to learn to "feel" them. This can be accomplished (as shown below) by playing two sets of 8th note triplets using alternate picking-and then two more sets of the same BUT miss the string with the up strokes of the pick.

(Tap the foot in 4 while playing this exercise-keep at it 'til you can "feel" the ♩ ♩ ♩)

* * * *

You are now able to read and play in five major keys in the second position. Actually you can now play in five (major) keys in any position by using these same fingerings (types - 1, 1A, 2, 3, 4) on the higher frets.

Example: Position II   Maj. keys C - F - G - D - A,

      Position III   C♯/D♭ - F♯/G♭ - A♭ - E♭ - B♭

Of course you can not yet read in these higher positions as you have not seen the notes that correspond to these fingering patterns in any area of the fingerboard but the second position.

On the following pages are shown the most used keys in the third position, first position (closed fingering-no open strings) and fourth position. You will be able to concentrate more on the notes as, by now, your "fingers should know the patterns".

Major Scales in 3rd Position
(MOST USED)

Bb MAJOR (FINGERING TYPE 4)

Eb MAJOR (FINGERING TYPE 3)

fine

Ab MAJOR (FINGERING TYPE 2)

Db MAJOR (FINGERING TYPE 1)

Double flat lowers
note 1 tone

Cancellation
reminder-back to
Bb as in signature

fine

3rd Position Review

OPTIONAL DUET WITH RHYTHM GUITAR

(Employing the four preceding Major Scales in Position III)

When played as a duet: 1.) Melody guitar as written-Rhythm guitar optional Latin Beat...   2.) Melody guitar play consecutive 8th notes as ♩♪ -Rhythm guitar straight 4.

TYPE 2

TYPE 1

fine

Chord Forms

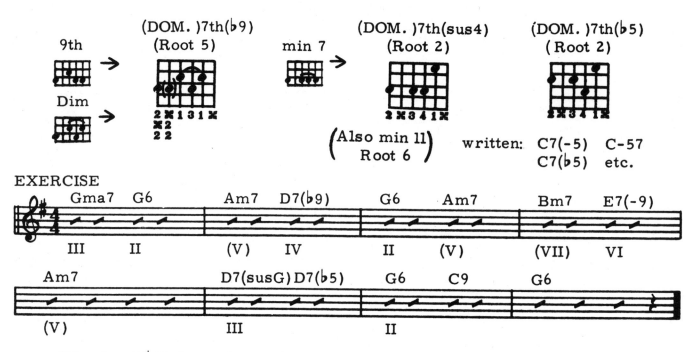

(Also min 11)
Root 6

written: C7(-5)   C-57
          C7(♭5)   etc.

EXERCISE

(The dom7(♭5) form shown above may also be named from the 6th string).

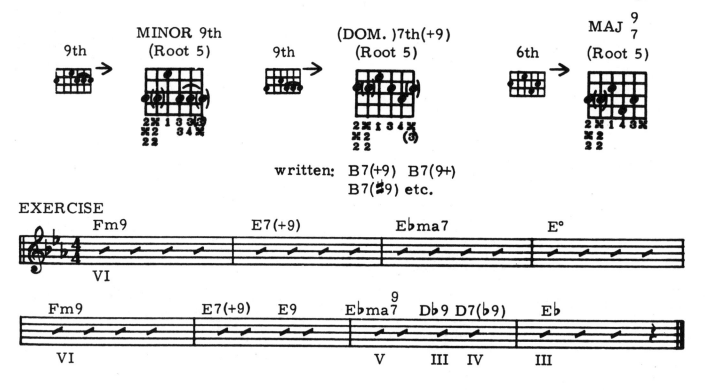

written: B7(+9)   B7(9+)
          B7(♯9) etc.

EXERCISE

The +9 chord used above would be called: E7th sharp 9.....E7th raise 9.....
or E7th augmented 9th.   This explicit reference to the altered degree is
important.....

Major Scales in 1st Position (no open strings)
(MOST USED)

Ab MAJOR (FINGERING TYPE 4)

Db MAJOR (FINGERING TYPE 3)

1st Position Review
OPTIONAL DUET WITH RHYTHM GUITAR
(Employing the two preceding Major Scales in Position I)

Melody guitar play consecutive 8th notes as written and as
Rhythm guitar play waltz beat for both

118   Ritard--   fine

Major Scales in 4th Position
(MOST USED)

G MAJOR (FINGERING TYPE 1A)

D MAJOR (FINGERING TYPE 1)

A MAJOR (FINGERING TYPE 2)

E MAJOR (FINGERING TYPE 3)

120

Chord Forms

(Substitution tip: ♭5 and +5 forms are almost always interchangeable - also +9 and ♭9).

4th Position Review
OPTIONAL DUET WITH RHYTHM GUITAR

(Employing the four preceding Major Scales in Position IV)

Melody guitar play consecutive 8th notes as written and as ♪³♪
Rhythm guitar play waltz beat for both

TYPE 1a

TYPE 1

Chord Forms

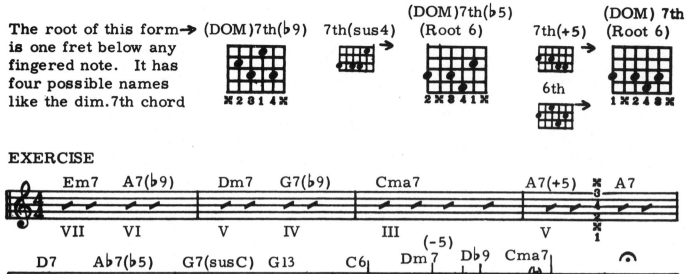

The root of this form→ is one fret below any fingered note. It has four possible names like the dim.7th chord

EXERCISE

| Em7 | A7(♭9) | Dm7 | G7(♭9) | Cma7 | A7(+5) | A7 |
| VII | VI | V | IV | III | V | |

| D7 | A♭7(♭5) | G7(susC) | G13 | C6 | Dm7(-5) | D♭9 | Cma7 |
| III | | | | I | III♭ | | |

Author's Notes

All forms presented in this book that employ the 6th string (and therefore sound in part in the real bass register) have the root (first) or fifth chordal degrees sounding on the bottom. These are the "strongest" chord tones and ALWAYS SOUND RIGHT.

You have probably seen some of these same forms elsewhere with different chord names indicated. Theoretically these other names are also correct: however, the bass notes are "weak" chordal degrees and require special handling. This will be discussed thoroughly in a later section...until then be careful of any forms that use the 6th string and do not have the root or fifth in the bass as they DO NOT always sound right.

In an orchestral rhythm part the chord symbols used generally indicate the total or complete harmonic structures and it is not expected (nor is it possible) that you play all degrees at all times. Of course you should try to play as close as possible to the written sequences, but actually simplification by OMITTING some of the chordal degrees is the "norm". (It is best, for now, to omit the higher degrees.)

Examples:	for C7+5(♭9) you may play:	C7(+5) (omit the ♭9) or:	C+
	for G7 ($^{13}_{-9}$) you may play:	G7(-9) (omit the 13th) or:	G7
	for F9(sus4) you may play:	F7(sus4) (omit the 9th)	

Be very careful of substitutions as they must be COMPLETELY compatible with the chord(s) indicated. (More about this later...)

Now, in addition to the five major keys in the second position, you should be somewhat familiar with the most used major scales in positions one, three and four. You will have to do a great deal of reading in these areas, however, to really know them.

I cannot over-emphasize the importance of learning the four major scale fingering types well as they are the foundation for other kinds of scales. We will gradually add more (major) fingering patterns (until, ultimately, we have twelve; one for each key in each position)...while at the same time we learn how to CONVERT PREVIOUSLY PRACTICED major forms into Jazz Minor, Harmonic Minor, etc.--

Our next project (Modern Method for Guitar, Part II) will be to learn the notes on the entire fingerboard by using all fingering types IN THE SAME KEY. This will require moving from position to position as we go through the patterns. The sequence of patterns (fingering types) will vary, depending upon the key signature. You will have a definite advantage in learning the fingerboard in this manner, as your "fingers know the patterns" and you can concentrate on the notes.

Remember: learning to play the guitar is an accumulative process--therefore regular, complete review is absolutely necessary for the gradual improvement and perfection of the techniques...

Index

RIGHT HAND DEVELOPMENT

SCALES - OPEN (FIRST) POSITION

SCALES - MOVABLE FINGERINGS (POSITION PLAYING)

SOLOS

SPEED STUDIES